PICKLES'
Illustrated

PICKLES, ILLUSTRATED

A Cookbook of 36 Recipes and Briny Miscellany

BY KAREN SOLOMON | ILLUSTRATIONS BY ALICE OEHR

CHRONICLE BOOKS
SAN FRANCISCO

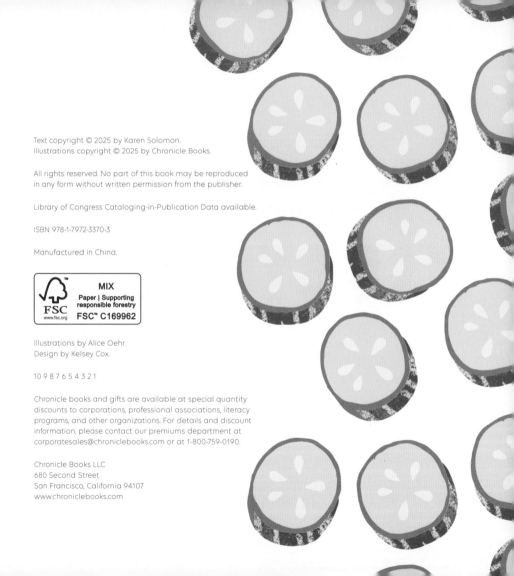

Library of Congress Cataloging-in-Publication Data available.

ISBN 978-1-7972-3370-3

Manufactured in China.

FSC
www.fsc.org

MIX
Paper | Supporting
responsible forestry
FSC™ C169962

Illustrations by Alice Oehr.
Design by Kelsey Cox.

10 9 8 7 6 5 4 3 2 1

Chronicle books and gifts are available at special quantity
discounts to corporations, professional associations, literacy
programs, and other organizations. For details and discount
information, please contact our premiums department at
corporatesales@chroniclebooks.com or at 1-800-759-0190.

Chronicle Books LLC
680 Second Street
San Francisco, California 94107
www.chroniclebooks.com

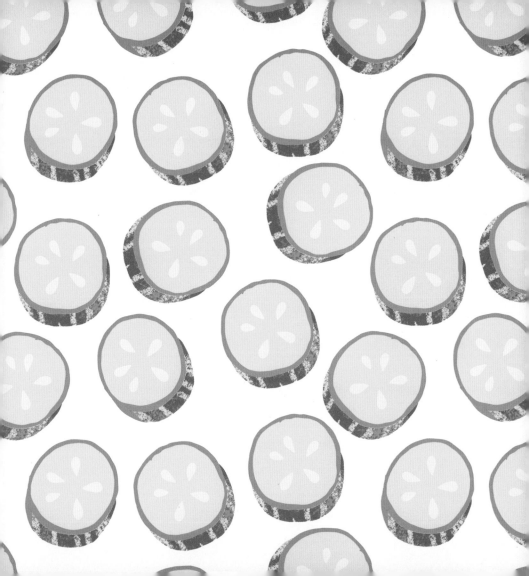

CONTENTS

INTRODUCTION · 8

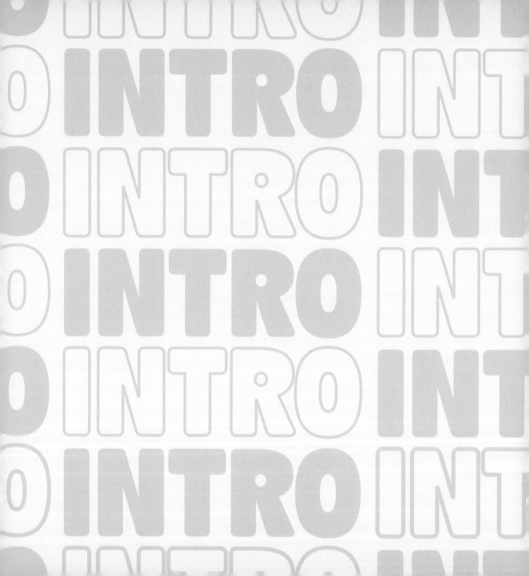

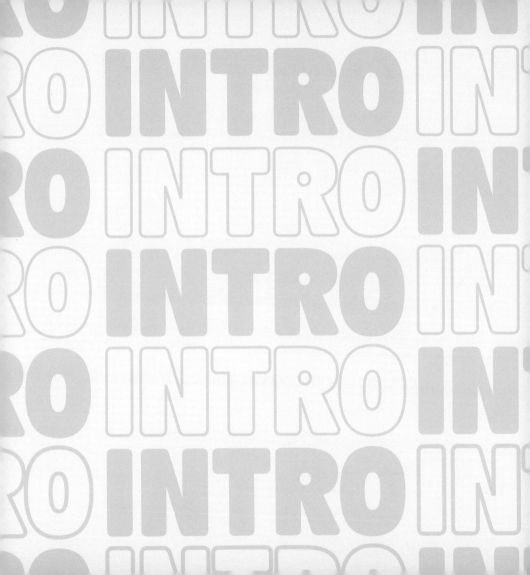

For many people, pickles are a side dish, a condiment, or an afterthought. But for me pickles are the main event, a way of life.

When you cook a meal, you eat it once, maybe twice if you're lucky. Pickling has its own kind of magic: When you stock your fridge with jars of delicious things that amplify every other dish, you can reap the benefits of your culinary creativity for weeks to come.

Coming home from the farmers' market with totes stuffed full of seasonal fruits and veggies is a feeling unlike any other. Preserving that bounty for days, weeks, or months is tremendously gratifying.

If this is your first foray into food preservation, know that I have tried my best to swing open all the gates for you.

But first, a pickling crash course. In short, there are four methods of preserving we're going to use in this book:

QUICK PICKLES, OR QUICKLES—This process entails chopping something watery into small pieces, dousing it with an acid (usually vinegar) and other flavor agents, and then letting it sit for 30 minutes or so before eating.

REFRIGERATOR PICKLES—The most common variety of pickle is made by chopping large or small pieces of any kind of fruit or vegetable and covering them with acid and salt to help draw out their moisture. If kept properly chilled, these can last for weeks or even months.

FERMENTATION—This method uses salt, liquid, and pressure to create an oxygen-free environment that lets the natural microbes in the air acidify, sour, and preserve a food.

SALT-CURING—Heavy doses of salt add flavor and work to extract moisture from vegetables, fruit, meat, or fish. When pressure is added to reduce oxygen and then prevent spoilage, salt-cured foods such as olives or salmon undergo transformations in flavor, texture, and longevity.

It's not uncommon to use more than one of these methods. Some recipes call for salt-curing, then acid. Others require that you ferment foods a bit before adding vinegar. The only limits are the edges of your flavor imagination.

Know also that this book eschews hot water bath canning and pressure canning preservation techniques. If you have a 40-acre farm and grow 100 pounds of, well, anything, then those tried-and-true methods of food storage that date back to the Napoleonic era can be a godsend to help stock your larder for the lean winter months. But in the days of modern canning—meaning an ample food supply, electricity, and small-batch recipes—the refrigerator is the best and safest way to store pickles. Most of the recipes you'll find here make just a few jars—the perfect amount for storing, sharing, and eating. Now, a couple of ground rules as we buckle up for our voyage down The Great Pickle Highway.

When I mention using a canning jar in a recipe, I opt for a glass canning jar. I like them because they won't retain odors and tend to have a good, tight-fitting lid. I also like how their sizes are standardized—half-pint, pint, quart, et cetera. Oh, and if you use a canning jar, it will make your pickles just look more like, uh, pickles—but that's just an added bonus. It's not a necessity, and an old sour cream container or food storage container will work just fine in a pinch.

A few of the fermented pickle recipes in here also give you the option to use a pickling crock. They can be great to work with—they're made of thick ceramic, which stays nice and cool, and some of them come with weights perfectly fitted for the vessel to help the pickle compress and exude the vegetable's natural liquids. However, I don't want crock ownership to be a barrier to pickling. They can be expensive and can take up a lot of space. And you can certainly make delicious pickles without one. Do not feel pressured to run out and buy a pickling crock. But if you have one, go to town! Hint: if you have a crock pot, the ceramic insert can function beautifully as a pickling crock.

Anytime sugar is used in these recipes, I am using granulated or cane sugar unless otherwise noted.

And salt. Let's talk about that. I specify different types of salt in each recipe. Not all salt is the same, and salts are not interchangeable. If I say Diamond Crystal Kosher Salt and you veer off into fine grain sea salt, you're going to have some very salty pickles.

While there are some more challenging recipes for weekend warriors looking for a real project, I have tried to keep the path to pickles smooth and accessible. Many recipes here are short and sweet (or spicy!). Ingredient lists and techniques have been distilled into only what's necessary. I want to stretch your vision of what can be considered a pickle with a few curveball ingredients—I'm looking at you, burdock root and green strawberries—but there are plenty of familiar points of entry for the common cucumber and a head of cabbage as well.

The book is organized around four flavor profiles: somewhat sour, kinda savory, roughly sweet, and mildly or wildly spicy. But again, this is not a closed system, and there is a lot of crossover between each category. Take the power in your own hands to tone down the heat, ramp up the sweetness, or add volume to the piquancy as you and the people you feed see fit.

Most importantly, remember that pickles are fun, funky, maybe even a little silly at times. Have fun. Enjoy yourself. Be gentle with yourself if you're new to cooking altogether. And above all, have fun.

Happy pickling!

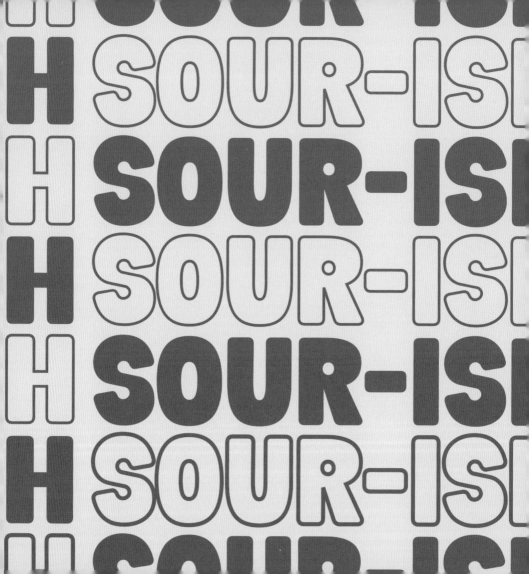

Fermented Brussels Sprouts

Think of this as sauerkraut in miniature. Teeny-tiny cabbage heads left whole retain quite a bit of crunch. And the best part? You may just feel like a giant while eating them.

This recipe is like a blank canvas, ready to receive any additional flavorings that your imagination can conjure, such as celery seeds, ajwain seeds, cumin seeds, juniper berries, or mustard seeds.

First, prepare **½ pound [230 g] of Brussels sprouts**. With the root end up, slice each one in half from bottom to top. Remove the tough outer leaves and discard them. Pack the Brussels sprouts into a pint jar along with **2 lightly crushed garlic cloves** and **1 tablespoon of black peppercorns**.

cont'd.

In a separate pourable container, combine **¼ cup [40 g] of kosher salt** with 1 quart [960 ml] of water until it makes a cloudy brine.

Pour the brine over the Brussels sprouts. The vegetables will want to float: Add a weight at the top of the jar to prevent them from doing so, such as a tightly sealed bag full of water or a clean rock—something just heavy enough to fully submerge the vegetables.

Cover the jar with a clean kitchen towel and secure it with string or a rubber band. This will let air in but keep debris and insects out. Leave the jar out in a cool, dark space while the Brussels sprouts ferment.

After a few days, you will notice some small natural fermentation bubbles and a "pickled" aroma. Check the top of the jar periodically for white mold, which should be removed and discarded.

Taste one of the Brussels sprouts after about 10 days. (They may ferment faster in warmer weather, but since these are pretty tough vegetables, you should give them at least 5 days.) Let your pickles go longer if you'd like them to get sourer and more tender.

When the Brussels sprouts are ready, remove the towel, put the lid on tightly, and put the jar in the refrigerator. They'll keep for several months, but the flavor and texture will continue to evolve.

Chowchow

This is a finely chopped relish hailing from the American South. Ingredients vary, depending on the family recipe (or if it's a northern variation), but chowchow almost always contains red bell peppers, onions, and cabbage. And if it's Southern style, it probably also has green tomatoes. Chowchow can be viciously sweet, but I've lightened up on the sugar here to let the sour brine sing. Spoon this next to grilled or roasted meats of any kind (hello, hot dogs and hamburgers), on top of a green salad, or into a potato salad for a piquant kick.

Use the pulse function on your food processor to finely chop **1 large white onion**, **½ of a head of cabbage**, **1 medium green bell pepper**, and **1 medium red bell pepper**. Pulse until the vegetables are roughly pea-size; be careful not to over-pulse. You should end up with roughly 2 cups [480 g] of each vegetable.

cont'd.

In a large mixing bowl, combine the chopped vegetables with **¼ cup [40 g] of kosher salt**. Cover and let the vegetables macerate to release their liquid overnight or for at least 6 hours.

Drain the vegetables and rinse them under cold water. Drain them again thoroughly and pack them into canning jars or any container with a tight-fitting lid.

Make the brine. In a medium saucepan, boil **1½ cups [300 g] of sugar**, **2 teaspoons of yellow mustard seeds**, **1 teaspoon of celery seeds**, **1 teaspoon of ground turmeric**, **2 cups [480 ml] of distilled white vinegar**, and 1 cup [240 ml] of water. Stir frequently to dissolve and distribute the spices.

Pour the boiling brine over the vegetables and put the lid on the jar. Let it sit at room temperature for a day, then refrigerate the relish for at least 2 days before eating it. Chowchow will keep for several weeks if refrigerated.

Pickled Red Onion

Here is a classic pickle to always have on hand. I like to pour boiling water over the onions to mellow them out and make them less sharp, but if you love onions full throttle then feel free to skip this step. Try this pickle on top of any kind of taco, next to a rich vindaloo and basmati, mixed in with potato or egg salad, or layered into a game-day monster sub sandwich.

Bring a medium saucepan of water to a boil. Slice **½ of a large red onion (about 6 ounces [170 g])** into ¼ inch [6 mm] thick strips.

cont'd.

Toss the onion strips into boiling water for 20 seconds. Drain them immediately and run them under cold water, tossing them with your hands to cool them down and stop the cooking. Drain the onions thoroughly.

Transfer the onions to a small mixing bowl. Add **¼ cup [20 g] of fresh cilantro leaves**, **1 teaspoon of kosher salt**, and **3 tablespoons of fresh lemon juice**. Toss thoroughly to combine.

You can serve this pickle immediately or you can cover it and keep it refrigerated for at least a week. As it sits, the flavors will mellow, and the onions will become softer and more pliable.

Water Kimchi

Though it has "kimchi" in the name, this is not the wildly fiery red cabbage you may be thinking of. In fact, this pickle has a delicate, summery flavor, which means you can also consume the brine as a drink or cold soup. Efficient, huh? Though this is not the longest-lasting dish, it's easy and quick, so you can make it as often as you like. Some say it's even good for hangovers.

Prepare the vegetables. **Peel 1 or 2 daikon radishes**, enough for about 2½ cups [370 g]. Cut them into quarters lengthwise and then into thin slices.

Cut **1 pound [455 g] of napa cabbage heads** lengthwise and chop them into 1 inch pieces. Cut **½ of a sweet apple** [about ¾ cup] first into quarters and then into thin slices. Peel **2 carrots** and cut them into thin half-moons (about 1¼ cups [40g]).

cont'd.

In a large mixing bowl, combine the vegetables with **2 tablespoons of fine sea salt**, **2 thinly sliced garlic cloves**, and a minced **1 inch piece of fresh ginger**.

Toss well and let the vegetables sit for 30 minutes, stirring once halfway through. The salt will draw out some of the moisture.

Toss the vegetables again and pack them into a 6-cup [1.4 L] ceramic or glass container.

In a separate pourable container, dissolve **1 teaspoon of Korean red chili flakes** and **1 tablespoon of sugar** into 4 cups [945 ml] of water. Pour the liquid over the vegetables until they are covered. Fill a tightly sealed plastic bag with water, secure it, and use it as a ballast over the top to keep the vegetables submerged below the liquid.

Cover the jar loosely and allow this pickle to sit in a cool, dark place for about 3 days; small fermentation bubbles will begin to surface. Once it has fermented lightly, put the lid on the jar tightly and refrigerate. It will keep for about 2 weeks.

Serve this kimchi and its delicious brine in a small bowl alongside a bowl of rice and your favorite protein.

PICKLE FACT

Too much pickle juice goes down the drain. It's not a leftover. It's a precious and flavorful kitchen resource that should be stored and savored. Here are a few ideas for what to do with leftover pickle juice:

- Reuse it! If it still has a strong flavor and some acidity, throw in fresh vegetables and a bit more salt to make refrigerator pickles.

- Use it anytime you'd usually reach for vinegar, including as a salad dressing or marinade, in potato salad or tuna salad, or as a

finishing sauce for cooked
meat or vegetables.

- Boil baby potatoes, cauliflower, or carrots in it
  for extra flavor.

- Slip it into a piquant
  cocktail instead of citrus
  juice. If you have not
  tried a Bloody Mary with
  pickle juice, you have
  not lived. You also can't
  go wrong with a pickle
  juice martini.

- Splash a little on your
  hydrangeas or azaleas or
  other acid-loving gar-
  den flowers to help them
  produce pretty colors and
  stay nourished.

Preserved Lime Pickle

This Indian pickle has a deep sourness meant to cleanse the palate. This is not a pickle you eat by the bowlful. One or two of these alongside rice and a rich coconut or lamb curry really perks up your mouth. These will last in the fridge for years and, like a fine wine, get better with age. As the pickle breaks down, an occasional shake to redistribute the liquid that falls to the bottom will help promote even fermentation.

Wash **10 small limes** and dry them.

cont'd.

In a medium skillet, heat **1 teaspoon of vegetable oil** over medium heat. Add the whole limes and sear their skins, rolling them around in the pan for even cooking, for 5 minutes. It's okay if the limes get brown in spots.

Transfer the cooked limes to a clean kitchen towel and let them cool until they can be handled. Use the towel to rub off the oil from the skin (or else they will be slippery under the knife). Chop each lime into about 16 small pieces.

Transfer the limes to a quart jar (or some other transparent container with a good lid). Add **3 tablespoons of kosher salt**, and shake the jar to evenly distribute the salt over the limes. Cover the jar loosely, place it in a sunny window, and let it sit for 4 days. Shake the limes daily to redistribute the salt. It's normal for a thick juice to leach from the fruit.

Now, make the brine. In a medium skillet over medium heat, warm **¼ cup [60 ml] of vegetable oil** and stir in **4 teaspoons of ground cayenne pepper**, **1 teaspoon of ground turmeric**, **2 teaspoons of asafetida**, and **2 teaspoons of ground coriander**. Cook for 3 minutes, stirring frequently, until fragrant. Add **2 teaspoons of black mustard seeds** and **2 teaspoons of yellow mustard seeds** and, stirring constantly, cook for about 1 minute more until the seeds begin to pop. Remove the skillet from the

cont'd.

heat, and mix in the fermented limes and all their juice along with **3 tablespoons of light brown sugar**. Stir well until the sugar is dissolved.

Pack the lime pickle back into the jar, cover it loosely with a towel or a lid, and let it sit at room temperature for 1 day. Refrigerate the jar for at least a week before tasting the pickles. Shake the jar every other day for the first couple of weeks, and then on occasion, and continue to store it in the refrigerator. Your lime pickle will last for at least a year.

Torshi

Across a broad swath of the preserved-food world—the Middle East, Armenia, Afghanistan—pickles are known as torshi, and this recipe is a mix of those traditions. They can vary dramatically in flavor, texture, appearance, and ingredients—just like the word "pickle" means a hundred different things in Western cuisine. A few common threads between torshi include big chunks of vegetables (carrots, cabbage, or peppers) combined with pre-pickled vegetables, such as jars of hot peppers, jarred pickles, pickled artichoke, olives, and more. Torshi pop with big flavors like garlic and chili, as well as coriander, allspice, and bay leaves.

cont'd.

Prepare the vegetables. Cut **2 medium carrots** and **2 celery stalks** into batons the size of French fries. Chop **½ of a small head of cabbage** into 1½ to 2 inch chunks. Peel and cut **2 medium turnips** into 8 half-moons. Slice **1 medium green pepper** into long strips. Cut **8 pickled pepperoncini** into ½ inch rings. Pack all the vegetables, along with **3 crushed garlic cloves** and **10 sprigs of parsley**, into a large jar or any container with a tight-fitting lid.

Make the brine. In a medium saucepan, boil 2 cups [480 ml] of water. Stir in **3 cups [720 ml] of apple cider vinegar**, **¼ cup [40 g] of kosher salt**, **2 teaspoons of yellow mustard seeds**, **2 teaspoons of coriander seeds**, **2 teaspoons of caraway seeds**, **1 teaspoon of black peppercorns**, **1 teaspoon of crushed red chili flakes**, **2 bay leaves**, and **3 cloves**. Allow the mixture to reach a rapid boil—cook just long enough to dissolve the spices.

Pour the boiling liquid over the vegetables and press down on them to submerge them below the brine line. Cover the jar loosely with its lid and let the pickles sit at room temperature for 24 hours, then move to the refrigerator. Let the torshi sit for at least 5 days before eating it. Covered and refrigerated, it will keep at least 2 months.

Savory Citrus Pickled Cabbage

Cabbage is universally enjoyed in some kind of preserved or salted state. Here, with the Southeast Asian flavors of lime juice, fish sauce, garlic, ginger, and chile, is one of my all-time favorites. Not only can this dish fill the void of any coleslaw at a picnic (thinking of you, fellow mayonnaise haters), but I also recommend you try it with stir-fried noodles or barbecued pork, chicken, or fish.

Discard the tough outer leaves of a **1½ pound [230 g] napa cabbage**. Lay the cabbage on its side with the root end facing you. Use a knife to split the root and then pull the cabbage apart into halves. Lay each half flat-side down and split the root again. You'll finish with four long spears of cabbage still held together by the root. Then chop the

cont'd.

cabbage quarters into 1 inch [2.5 cm] pieces, discarding the core and root, and transfer the pieces to a large mixing bowl. Rub **2 tablespoons of kosher salt** into the cabbage and let it sit for 20 minutes. Stir it once halfway through; you'll notice that the cabbage will start to wilt and appear wet.

While the cabbage sits, squeeze **½ cup [120 ml] of fresh lime juice** from about 5 limes. Mince **1 large garlic clove** and a **1 inch [2.5 cm] cube of peeled fresh ginger**. Slice **1 small jalapeño** into very thin rounds.

Squeeze the wilted cabbage hard to rid it of some of its water and salt. Drain it and return it to the bowl.

Add the lime juice, garlic, ginger, and jalapeño to the cabbage along with **3 tablespoons of fish sauce** and **1 tablespoon of sugar**. Mix thoroughly to combine.

You can eat this pickle right away, but it's best to let it marinate for at least a day (you can do so in the mixing bowl or transfer the pickle to a canning jar). When covered tightly and stored in the refrigerator, this pickle will last at least 3 weeks.

PICKLE FACT

Pickling cucumbers have a rooting hormone at the tip that, if not removed, will render your pickles mushy. Before making any kind of cucumber pickle, be sure to wash them thoroughly and use a small paring knife to remove the differently colored tips to keep your pickles crisp.

Also, since we're talking cukes—salad cucumbers are good for salad and quick pickles, but not for long-term storage because they're too watery. Look for smaller pickling cucumber varieties like Kirbys or Persians, which are more dense and less watery and will therefore stay crisper longer.

Kosher Dills

When people close their eyes and think of a cartoon image of a pickle, they're thinking of a kosher dill. These beauties are bursting with everything you'd expect from the accompaniment to your pastrami sandwich; they're briny with a naturally created tanginess. This is the recipe to master as a budding pickler. To customize it, feel free to add in a teaspoon or so of celery seeds, cumin seeds, dill seeds, juniper berries, and/or mustard seeds.

Prepare **2 pounds [910 g] of Kirby, Persian, or other small pickling cucumbers**. Scrub them well under running water, particularly at the root end, to prevent soggy pickles.

cont'd.

In the bottom of a glass jar or crock that's big enough to hold all the cucumbers, place **3 lightly crushed garlic cloves**, **2 tablespoons of black peppercorns**, and **1 bunch of fresh dill**. Pack the cucumbers on top of the spices tightly, standing them upright when you can and shoving them in like sardines in a can.

In a separate pitcher, combine **¼ cup [40 g] kosher salt** with 1 quart [960 ml] of water until it makes a cloudy brine. Pour the brine over the cucumbers until they are completely covered in liquid (even if it means mixing up a second batch of brine).

The cukes will want to float. Prevent them from doing so by adding weight (such as a tightly sealed bag full of water or a large, clean rock) on top of the vegetables to fully submerge them in the brine.

Cover the jar or crock with a clean kitchen towel and secure it with string or a rubber band. This will let air in but keep debris and insects out. Let the jar or crock sit in a cool, dark place.

After a few days, you will start to notice some small natural fermentation bubbles and a "pickled" aroma. If you see a bit of white mold at the top, remove it and discard. Keep checking for mold every couple of days.

Taste your pickles after about 10 days (vegetables will ferment faster in warmer weather, and larger vegetables take longer to ferment). Let your pickles go longer if you'd like them to get sourer (note that they will continue to sour and soften, albeit more slowly, once they've moved to the fridge). Some people let them go for weeks for a really tangy taste.

When your kosher dills are ready to eat, put the lid on the jar and refrigerate. These will keep refrigerated for several months.

▼

Sauerkraut

Hard to spell, easy to make and eat, this is the quintessential fermented pickle. I consider sauerkraut to be one of the hardest-working pickles in the pickle business. Why? It's mild, crunchy, and tastes great alone or as a side dish, on a sandwich, cooked into soups, or alongside sausage sizzling in a pan. And this baby is versatile! Swap out a pound of the cabbage with crisp, tart apples, shredded carrot, and/or thinly sliced red onion at the bottom of the crock (to help the onion keep its bright color). Don't let the short ingredient list fool you. This recipe is all about technique. And hey—the upper body workout is free.

cont'd.

Thoroughly clean and dry a 1 gallon [3.8 L] ceramic crock (you could already have one as the insert in your slow cooker) or a food-grade, BPA-free plastic bucket. Measure out **3 table-spoons of fine-grain sea salt** into a small dish. Quarter, core, and slice **5 pounds [2.3 kg] of green cabbage heads** into ¼ inch [6 mm] strips.

Scatter a pinch of the salt onto the bottom of the crock. Start adding the cabbage a little at a time, punching it down firmly and layering it with the salt. Reserve about 2 teaspoons of the salt for later.

Using your fist or a blunt implement—the edge of a rolling pin, a meat tenderizer, the handle of a hammer wrapped in plastic—bruise the cabbage by stabbing it all over in an up-and-down motion. You want to decrease the volume by about one-third. And, most importantly, you want to make sure the cabbage is very wet and juicy at the surface when pressed. This takes about 10 minutes, so be patient, and take pleasure in working out your frustrations!

Use your hands to flatten the surface of the cabbage and scrape any leaves from the side of the crock or bucket. Press the cabbage down tightly to release as much air as possible. Sprinkle the remaining salt over the top, especially around the edges where the cabbage meets the container, as this is the most likely place where mold could occur.

Gently lay a sheet of plastic wrap over the surface of the cabbage, but do not make it airtight.

Over the plastic wrap, lay a flat plate or pot lid. It should be round and large enough to cover the surface of the cabbage almost entirely, but it should not touch the sides of the crock or bucket. As the cabbage wilts and settles, the lid should be able to drop down and stay on top of the cabbage without getting stuck on the sides of the container.

Place an object that weighs at least 2 pounds [910 g] on top of the plate or lid to add pressure. Some tools for this job could include large, clean rocks, a hand weight, a large jar filled with water, or a heavy stack of cans.

Cover the container with cheesecloth or a thin cotton kitchen towel. Secure the fabric with a string or large rubber band to let air flow in and keep out insects and debris.

Keep the container in a cool place away from direct sunlight. Check it the next day; the surface should be wet and juicy when you press down on the weight. (If it's dry, bruise the cabbage some more until liquid appears.)

cont'd.

The sauerkraut should sit out and ferment for at least 1 week. The longer it sits, the more fermented it will become. Be sure to check it at least every other day to make sure the surface remains moist and mold free. If you do find small amounts of white mold (and you probably will; it's quite common), simply scoop them away and discard them.

Your sauerkraut can sit for at least 3 weeks. But don't forget about it! Keep checking it every few days to remove small bits of mold and to make sure all solid pieces of cabbage remain wet and completely below the brine line. It's ready to eat when you like the aroma; it will smell pleasantly sour and tangy.

Once you're ready to enjoy and/or store it, stir the sauerkraut thoroughly from top to bottom to help distribute the salt and other flavors.

Store it in the refrigerator, either in the crock you've used for fermenting (if it has a tight lid) or in jars or containers with lids. Be sure to pack the containers tightly, with all vegetables scraped away from the sides and submerged in the liquid. If properly stored, it will keep for weeks, and it will continue to ferment slowly and evolve its flavor and texture. If it sits for too long it can become soft and mushy—but that makes it great for cooking into soups and stews. If small bits of white mold appear on it while it's in the fridge, just scrape them away and eat the rest of the pickle.

Pink Pickled Turnips

Don't sleep on this little mood lifter. Iridescently pink and irresistible, this lightly fermented and marinated pickle is crunchy, perfect on a falafel, and a staple of many Middle Eastern diets. While these turnips are often served with cracked olives, pita, dips, and spreads, I encourage you to reach for this anytime you'd use fresh celery: Give it a go in an egg salad, a tuna salad, or a pasta salad for some pretty, pickled crunch.

Peel and cut **2 pounds [910 g] of turnips** and **1 small red beet** into ¼ inch [6 mm] half-moons. Pack them into a large canning jar or another container with a tight-fitting lid.

cont'd.

In a medium saucepan, boil 3 cups [720 ml] of water with **⅓ cup [55 g] of kosher salt**, **1 large bay leaf**, and **1 cup [240 ml] of distilled white vinegar**.

Pour the brine over the vegetables. Cover the jar loosely with the lid and let the pickle sit at room temperature for 1 week. Once done, the turnips can be refrigerated until ready to serve. They'll keep for at least 1 month, though eventually they'll get unpleasantly soft.

Pickled Burdock

Burdock root isn't common on the Western table, but it should be. It's mild and slightly sweet, and its texture is like that of a sunchoke or turnip. These long, brown logs boil up beautifully in soup (pickled or raw), and are terrific in any kind of stir-fried or boiled rice dish. As a pickle, burdock fully stands on its own alongside rice, meat, and fish. Burdock discolors very quickly—even faster than potatoes—but an acid bath can help it keep its creamy color.

Ready an acid bath. In a large bowl of cool water add **2 tablespoons of distilled white vinegar or the juice of half of a lemon**.

cont'd.

Chop **1 pound [455 g] of fresh burdock** into 4 inch [10 cm] lengths. Peel each piece of burdock. The woody, fibrous skin tends to run fairly deep, so take your time and get all of it. Transfer the peeled burdock to the acid bath. Then, working with one piece at a time, slice the burdock into thin circular coins, placing them back into the acid bath as you go.

Bring a medium saucepan of water to a boil. Remove the burdock coins from the acid bath, drain them, and transfer them to the saucepan. Boil the burdock coins for 7 to 10 minutes, stirring occasionally, until they are tender and sweet.

Drain the burdock coins well and pack them into a glass jar (like you're filling a jar with pennies). Combine **¾ cup [180 ml] of unseasoned rice vinegar**, **3 tablespoons of sugar**, and ¼ cup [60 ml] of water, and pour it over the burdock. Cover the jar loosely with its lid and let it sit at room temperature for 1 day before refrigerating. Your burdock is ready to eat, but it will taste even better after 3 days.

Cauliflower Ceviche

For this take on ceviche, ditch the fish and try it with fresh, crunchy cauliflower. After all, the best parts of ceviche are the unsung hero ingredients: bright lime juice, chile spice, and punchy garlic and onion. The biggest challenge here is squeezing all those fresh limes—you'll need 8 to 10 of them—so enlist some help in the kitchen to get this into your mouth ASAP.

Add **3 tablespoons of salt** to a large pot of water (about 6 cups) and bring that to a boil while you chop **2 small heads of cauliflower** into bite-size pieces.

cont'd.

Boil the cauliflower until it's just tender, about 3 to 5 minutes depending on the size of the pieces.

Drain the cauliflower and run it under cold water, tossing it gently, to stop the cooking. Drain it once again.

Prepare the rest of the ceviche. Dice **1 small red onion** and **2 jalapeños**. Finely mince **1 garlic clove**. Cut **1 pint [340 g] of cherry tomatoes** into quarters.

In a large mixing bowl, combine all ingredients with the cauliflower. Add **1 cup [240 ml] of fresh lime juice**, **1 cup [40 g] of packed, chopped cilantro**, and **1 tablespoon of kosher salt**.

Put the lid on the jar tightly and chill the ceviche for at least 2 hours, but overnight is better. Eat it on chips, tostadas, or crackers. Refrigerated, this will last at least 1 week.

Green Strawberry Salsa

The young, green, unripe berries that usually fill your jam jar are excellent for pickling, as is a lot of green fruit. The flavor and texture of a green strawberry is not unlike a tomatillo. I know it may be tricky to find these berries, but ask your local farmers' market strawberry vendor, and I'm sure they will be happy to bring you some.

I already know what you're thinking. Can you really call a salsa a pickle? I say yes. We are safely in the realm of food cured in acid for longer storage. This just so happens to be a pickle that tastes very good on chips.

cont'd.

Hull and dice **1 pint of unripe strawberries**. Chop ½ to ¾ of **1 red onion** (about ¾ cup [105 g]). Mince **3 garlic cloves**.

Add the strawberries, onions, and garlic to a medium saucepan along with **¼ cup [60 ml] of fresh lime juice**, **¼ cup [60 ml] of distilled white vinegar**, **1½ teaspoons of kosher salt**, and **½ teaspoon of cayenne pepper**. Cover and boil for about 5 minutes, stirring occasionally, until it becomes thick and saucy.

Remove from heat and allow the salsa to cool for about 10 minutes, stirring occasionally. Then stir in **½ cup [4 g] of fresh mint leaves** (tightly packed).

Your salsa is now chip ready. It will keep, refrigerated, for about 2 weeks.

PICKLE FACT

Fruit, as well as vegetables, can be pickled. Green tomatoes, green strawberries, peaches, apples, and watermelon rind are just some of the fruits that make delicious pickles.

Three Bean Salad

Don't tell anyone, but this throwback "salad" from relish trays of yore is really a pickle. And unlike most pickles based solely on vegetables, this one has the powerful protein punch of beans.

If you use homemade kidney beans and garbanzos, this will have a much better texture, but don't beat yourself up about using canned beans if that's what's convenient. Yellow wax beans will certainly make for a prettier color pop, but if you can't find them, just swap them out for green beans instead.

cont'd.

Prepare the beans. If you're using canned beans, drain them, rinse them, and measure out **2 cups [320 g] of red kidney beans** and **2 cups [320 g] of chickpeas**.

If you're starting with dry beans, soak 1 cup [160 g] (or more) of each of the dried beans overnight. Drain the beans and rinse them well. In two medium saucepans, add the soaked beans and enough fresh water to cover them by 2 inches [5 cm]. Bring the beans to a boil, then reduce the heat to simmer the beans for 60 to 75 minutes, until the beans are tender and cooked through. Measure out the beans for the recipe and save any remaining beans for another use.

In a medium Dutch oven, boil 8 cups [1.9 L] of water with **1 teaspoon of kosher salt**. Trim, wash, and cut **½ pound [230 g] of yellow wax beans or green beans** into 1 inch [6 mm] pieces. Boil them in the Dutch oven for 2 minutes. Drain the beans and run them under cold water to stop the cooking.

Chop **½ of a medium red onion** into bean-size pieces (about 1 cup [240 ml]). Chop **2 to 3 celery stalks** into bean-size pieces (about ¾ cup [180 ml]). Set aside.

Return the empty Dutch oven to the stove to make the brine. Combine **1½ cups [360 ml] of distilled white vinegar**, 2 cups [480 ml] of water, **¾ cup [150 g] of sugar**, and **1 tablespoon of**

kosher salt. Bring the brine to a boil and stir to dissolve the sugar. Remove from heat.

To the brine, add the kidney beans, chickpeas, green beans or wax beans, red onion, and celery. Stir to combine.

Pack the pickle mixture tightly into a ½-gallon [1.9 L] canning jar or any large container with a tight-fitting lid. Make sure the vegetables are covered with the brine completely, then add **½ cup [120 ml] of extra-virgin olive oil** at the top.

This pickle is best if it sits at least 1 hour before eating. It will keep, refrigerated, for at least 2 months.

Curtido

At the intersection of coleslaw and sauerkraut you will find curtido, the quintessential pickle of El Salvador. And it is difficult to eat pupusas without it. The name translates to "cut," a very simple way to describe this dish of lightly fermented cut cabbage. If you have a mandoline or a shredder extension on your food processor, this is the time to use it. If not, put that knife to work!

Curtido transforms over time. When fresh, it's light and crunchy like a crisp salad. But as it sits, marinates, and ferments, the vegetables get more tender, and its sour, fermented flavor gets more pronounced.

Boil about 6 cups [1.4 L] of water in a large pot (you'll need enough water to cover the vegetables by 2 inches [5 cm]).

cont'd.

Core and remove the outer leaves of **1 medium head of green cabbage** and cut the cabbage into thin slices (about 5 cups [450 g]). Cut **1 white onion** into very thin slices (about 1 cup [230 g]). Shred **1 to 2 large carrots** (about 1 cup [340 g]).

Combine all ingredients in a large mixing bowl and pour the boiling water over the vegetables until they are submerged. Let them sit for 1 minute, then drain the vegetables well and return them to the bowl.

Cut **1 medium jalapeño** into thin rings and add them to the bowl.

Grate the **zest of 1 lime** and add it to the bowl, along with **¼ cup [60 ml] of fresh lime juice**, **½ cup [120 ml] of apple cider vinegar**, **1 tablespoon of extra virgin olive oil**, **2 teaspoons of kosher salt**, **1 tablespoon of dried oregano**, and **1 teaspoon of freshly ground black pepper**. Stir to combine.

You can enjoy your curtido right away. To store, pack the pickle into jars or any container with a tight-fitting lid and keep refrigerated. Stir it well before serving. It will last at least 3 weeks.

Pickled Shrimp

Make this pickle when you're in despeate need of the "perfect bite." The onion and celery are meant to be eaten along with the shrimp on a cracker, with a couple shakes of hot sauce and/or a drizzle of EVOO if you're feeling adventurous. By all means, pack this baby up for a picnic or potluck. It travels well, feels kind of luxurious, and crosses the threshold into appetizer-ville when you want something more substantial than vegetables. You can use smaller shrimp if you wish. What's far more important than size is their freshness and quality.

In a medium saucepan, bring 6 cups [1.4 L] of water and **2 tablespoons of kosher salt** to a rapid boil. Drop **1 pound [455 g] of large shrimp, shelled and deveined**, into the water and cook them, stirring often, until they're completely curled (about 2 minutes, depending on the size of the shrimp).

cont'd.

Drain them, rinse them under cold running water to stop the cooking, and let them drain again and cool. Hang on to the pot, as we'll use it to make the brine.

Very thinly slice **1 large lemon** (about 10 paper-thin slices), **1 medium red onion** (about ¾ cup), and **2 to 3 celery stalks** (about ¾ cup).

In a medium mixing bowl, combine the shrimp and the lemon, onion, and celery slices with **2 teaspoons of black pepper-corns**, **4 dried bay leaves**, **4 whole cloves**, and **1 sprig of fresh tarragon**. Pack the mixture firmly into a quart canning jar or any container with a tight-fitting lid.

In the pot, combine **2 teaspoons of kosher salt** with ¾ **cup [180 ml] of apple cider vinegar**, ¾ cup [180 ml] of water, **1 large finely minced garlic clove**, and **2 tablespoons of sugar**. Heat until the mixture just starts to boil, stirring to dissolve the sugar and the salt.

Pour the brine over the packed shrimp and put the lid on the jar.

Allow the shrimp to marinate in the refrigerator for at least 4 hours, though overnight (or longer) is better. Fully submerged beneath the brine, this pickle will keep for at least 2 to 3 weeks. Note that if the shrimp sit too long, their flavor will remain, but their texture will soften.

Dilly Pickled Green Beans

These green beans are the Bloody Mary garnish that will knock off your cocktail socks. This little pickle also offers that critical acidic bite for pairing with meat or sausage of any kind. Take them to your next grill-fest and watch them disappear.

Trim and wash **¾ pound [340 g] of tender yet crisp green beans**.

In the bottom of a pint jar with a tight-fitting lid, place **1 lightly crushed garlic clove**, **1 tablespoon of dill seeds**, and **1 teaspoon of kosher salt**. Tilt the jar on its side and in it stand up 1 small bunch of fresh dill. Vertically pack as many green beans as possible into the jar; they should be like sardines in a can. If any beans are taller than the jar, snip them down to size.

cont'd.

Stand the jar upright. Fill it halfway with **distilled white vinegar**, and then top it off with water.

Put the lid on tightly, shake the jar gently to dissolve the salt, and refrigerate it. In 3 to 5 days, you'll have delicious pickles that will last for several months.

PICKLE FACT

Legend has it that Reggie Cunningham, a bartender at the Bushwick Country Club in Brooklyn, was the first to create the pickleback: a shot of pickle brine to follow a shot of whiskey. People love to debate food origin stories, and if you ask the internet, this is what you'll read. However, I must point out that in Mexico, long before Brooklyn hipsters were kickin' it with a pickleback, people were enjoying a shot of sangrita—a sweet, tangy, and often spicy blend of pickle brine and fruit juice—after a tequila shot.

Cold-Cured Salmon

If you rub high-quality fresh salmon with sugar and salt—guess what? Magic happens! The moisture is pulled from the fish to preserve it, and the texture becomes both silky and toothsome. It is ready for cream cheese and capers.

A few notes: One, do not skimp on the quality of the fish or the cut. The fish should be fresh and not previously frozen. And be sure to get a center cut (not a tail piece) so that it cures evenly. Two, when it comes time to slice and serve the salmon, make sure your knife is very, very sharp. A dull knife will just mash the fish to bits. Try as I might, I've yet to find a good use for the cured skin. If you have a way to make it delicious, please let me know.

cont'd.

Pat dry **1 pound [455 g] of fresh salmon** with paper towels. Lay down a double layer of plastic wrap and place the fish in the center, skin-side down.

In a small bowl, combine **3 tablespoons of kosher salt**, **3 tablespoons of sugar**, and **2 teaspoons of freshly ground black pepper**. Rub this mixture all over the flesh of the fish, including the sides, and use a small amount underneath on the skin. Scatter **1 bunch of fresh dill** on top of the fish to cover the top completely.

Wrap the fish tightly in the plastic wrap, pressing out any air bubbles. Then wrap it again to make an even tighter package. Place the wrapped fish inside a zip-top bag, pressing out as much air from the bag as possible.

Place the wrapped fish in a shallow dish, skin-side down, as it will release liquid as it cures. Place a flat 1 pound [455 g] weight on top of the fish, such as a dinner plate with a big bag of rice or beans on top. Allow the weighted fish to cure in the refrigerator for 3 days.*

Once cured, unwrap the fish and discard the dill and any extruded liquid. Pat it dry with paper towels.

To serve, slice long, thin pieces against the grain of the fish. I find it easiest to slice the whole thing at once, layering slices onto parchment paper or wax paper. For thinner slices, make sure your knife is very sharp and freeze the fish for 20 minutes first to firm it up.

Wrapped tightly in plastic wrap and refrigerated, this cured fish will keep for at least 2 weeks. Wrapped airtight it can be frozen for at least 3 months. In either case, it's best to keep the slices separated by parchment or wax paper. If you freeze it, also put the plastic-wrapped fish in a ziploc bag.

* While this fish is traditionally prepared and eaten cold, the National Center for Home Food Preservation recommends heating the fish to an internal temperature of 140°F [60°C].

If you opt to bake the salmon, place it on a rack over a baking sheet. Bake it in a 200°F [95°C] for about 20 minutes or until it reaches 140°F [60°C] at its thickest part. Note that baking the salmon will completely change its silky texture.

Bread and Butter Pickles

This is as basic as a basic pickle can be: spiced but pretty sweet, with a bit of crunch left in it, but flexible enough for your burger bun or sandwich. When you think of the ideal pickle, this could be it. I've dialed down the sugar a bit because I don't like my sweet pickles that sweet, but you are certainly invited to amplify it as needed.

Prepare the vegetables. Cut **2 to 2½ pounds [910 g to 1.1 kg] of Kirby cucumbers**, ends removed, into ¼ inch [6 mm] rounds until you have about 4 cups [140 g]. Cut **1 red onion** into thin slices until you have about 1 cup [140 g]. In a large mixing bowl, combine the cucumbers and onions with **¼ cup [40 g] of kosher salt**. Let the mixture

cont'd.

sit and macerate for 2 hours so that the salt draws moisture out of the vegetables. Toss them well and then drain the cucumber and onion thoroughly.

Pack the vegetables into jars or any container with a tight-fitting lid.

Make the brine. In a medium saucepan, bring **1 cup [240 ml] of apple cider vinegar**, **¾ cup [150 g] of sugar**, **1½ teaspoons of ground turmeric**, **2 teaspoons of yellow mustard seeds**, **1 teaspoon of coriander seeds**, **½ teaspoon of celery seeds**, and **1 teaspoon of red chili flakes** to a boil. Stir to dissolve the sugar and distribute the spices.

Pour the brine over the vegetables until they are fully sub-merged. Cover tightly. Let the jars sit at room temperature for 24 hours, and then move the pickles to the refrigerator. They're ready to eat after 3 days and they will last for at least 3 weeks.

Pickled Whole Cranberries

Spoon them alongside sliced turkey, float them in a champagne cocktail, skewer them to brighten up a cheese plate, or plunk them into a fruit salad—these bright, bursting, boba-like orbs are sweet, tangy, and tinged with warm spices to be enjoyed around the holidays and beyond. And guess what? They last for months in the fridge, meaning you can easily scale this recipe to have a quick hostess gift ready to share.

Sort and wash **1 cup [140 g] of fresh cranberries** and discard any shriveled or blemished fruit.

cont'd.

In the bottom of a half-pint jar, add a **½ inch thick slice of fresh ginger**, a **1 inch [6 mm] piece of lemon zest**, **1 star anise**, **½ cinnamon stick**, **1 clove**, **1 bay leaf**, and **½ teaspoon of kosher salt**. Then pack the cranberries into the jar without bruising them.

Now make the brine. In a small saucepan, boil **¼ cup [60 ml] of distilled white vinegar**, 2 tablespoons of water, and **½ cup [100 g] of sugar**, stirring to dissolve the sugar. Pour the boiling brine over the cranberries until they are submerged.

Put the lid on the jar and refrigerate. Let the cranberries sit for at least 5 days before eating them.

Cinnamon Clove Pickled Peaches

Fun fact: All pickled or canned peaches must be peeled, as the skins get tough and discolored. The fruit, however, is refreshing, tangy, sweet, and savory—the perfect multipurpose pickle.

Look for small-ish fresh peaches that are ripe but not too soft. Overly ripe fruit will get mushy after boiling and brining. And how, you may ask, should this pickle be eaten? With ice cream or pound cake on the sweet front. With roast chicken or turkey on the savory. Offer slices on a cheese plate next to aged cheddar, or better yet, layer it in a grilled cheese. This recipe makes 1 pint of pickles, but it's easily doubled if you find yourself flush with peaches.

cont'd.

Prepare **4 to 5 small peaches**. Wash them, cut them into quarters, and remove the pits. Place them in a medium saucepan.

Fill the saucepan with enough water to cover the peaches and ready an ice bath. Boil the peaches for 1 minute, then drop them into the ice bath until they're cool enough to handle. Remove and discard the skins. Hang on to the saucepan; we're going to use it again.

Stack the peaches snugly (but not squished) into a pint canning jar.

Make the brine. In the saucepan, combine **¼ cup [60 ml] of apple cider vinegar**, ¼ cup [60 ml] of water, **¼ cup [50 g] of sugar**, **½ teaspoon of kosher salt**, **¼ teaspoon of ground cinnamon**, and **3 cloves**. Bring it to a boil, stirring to dissolve the sugar. Pour the hot brine over the peaches until they are submerged.

Cover the jar tightly with the lid and let the peaches cool to room temperature. Move them to the refrigerator and let them sit for 1 week before tasting (it takes a few days for the peaches to fully soak up the brine). The peaches will keep, covered in brine and refrigerated, for at least 1 month.

PICKLE FACT

The idiom "in a pickle" has a few different meanings. Shakespeare is often credited with the phrase from *The Tempest* ("How came'st thou in this pickle?"), but his usage is more about being drunk—"pickled" with alcohol. The modern version of "in a pickle," meaning "in a difficult situation," probably comes from a Dutch phrase that translates to "sit in the pickle brine"—which would be quite a predicament with an unknown resolution, indeed.

Pickled Daikon Radish with Fresh Lemon

Daikon radish can be tricky to find outside of an Asian grocery store. But if you can get your hands on this mild, juicy, crunchy veg, know that you've found a goldmine of texture. It's versatile for soups and salads, it's comically oversized for a radish, and it has a clean, white flesh that just looks pretty on a plate. It's a pleasure to pickle since it cures quickly from its high water content and keeps its crunch. Eat this on top of rice and/or with a strong fish, like sardines or mackerel.

cont'd.

Peel and cut **1½ pounds [230 g] of daikon radish** into very thin slices. Transfer the daikon to a colander in or over the sink and toss the slices with **¼ cup [40 g] of kosher salt**. Let the daikon sit for 15 minutes, tossing occasionally.

In a medium bowl, whisk together **1 teaspoon of toasted sesame oil**, **1 tablespoon of honey**, **1 tablespoon of seasoned rice vinegar**, **⅓ cup [80 ml] of fresh lemon juice**, **1 minced garlic clove**, and **three 2 inch [5 cm] pieces of lemon zest**.

Rinse the daikon under running water to remove the salt, and drain it thoroughly. On a large, clean dish towel, spread the daikon out to dry, and gently roll up the slices to extract as much moisture as possible.

Add the daikon to the bowl and mix well, then pack the slices into a jar or a container with a tight lid. Pour in the brine, put the lid on the jar, and let it rest at room temperature for at least 1 hour before eating the pickles. These will keep in the refrigerator for up to 1 month. Shake the jar occasionally to evenly distribute the brine.

Fresh Apple Chutney

In contrast to the fresh chutney in the previous recipe, this spicy-and-sweet spoonable is designed to last longer. Like most Indian or British chutneys, this is outstanding with a sharp cheddar or, better still, on a grilled cheese. It can also be used as a pie filling solo, or you can just add a layer of it on the bottom of the pie under the apple filling.

In a small, heavy-bottomed Dutch oven over medium heat, dry-toast (stirring often) **1 tablespoon of cumin seeds**, **1 teaspoon of coriander seeds**, **2 teaspoons of Aleppo pepper (or red chili flakes)**, and **1 teaspoon of yellow mustard seeds** until the spices become fragrant and the cumin toasts to a light brown, about 3 to 5 minutes. Pour the spices into a

cont'd.

bowl to stop the cooking and let them cool. Grind them into a powder and set them aside.

Prepare the apples. Peel, core, and dice **5 large apples**. I like to mix sweet varieties, like Fujis, with tart apples, like Granny Smiths. Dice **½ of a red onion** and **1 small red bell pepper**.

Return the Dutch oven to the stove over medium-high heat. Add **⅓ cup [80 ml] of canola or grapeseed oil** and **2 teaspoons of kosher salt**, and cook the onion and peppers, stirring occasionally, until they're dark brown around the edges, about 12 minutes.

Reduce the heat to medium. Add half the chopped apples and ¼ cup [60 ml] of water to the Dutch oven and stir. Cover and let the apples tenderize, stirring occasionally, for about 5 minutes. Remove the lid and add the remaining apples, the ground spices, and **¼ cup [40 g] of brown sugar**, and stir frequently. Cook until some of the apples are very soft, and all of them are cooked through, about another 5 minutes.

Turn off the heat and stir the chutney. Add **½ cup [6 g] of lightly packed cilantro** and stir to combine.

The chutney can be served immediately or chilled. Covered and refrigerated, it will keep for at least 4 weeks.

Vietnamese Daikon and Carrot Pickle

If you've ever eaten a Vietnamese banh mi sandwich, then you are already well acquainted with the shredded pickle that is nestled between the meat and the cilantro. It's colorful, crunchy, and versatile: Take it for a test drive on a hot dog, a fish taco, or fried rice.

Peel **1 large carrot** and **half of 1 medium daikon radish**. Roughly shred the peeled vegetables in a food processor or by hand.

cont'd.

Transfer the shreds to a colander and toss them with **1 tablespoon of kosher salt**; use your hands to evenly work the salt into the vegetables. Pat the vegetables down tight; they will quickly start to exude lots of liquid. Let them sit for 10 minutes to draw out more moisture, then toss and squeeze them again.

Pack the vegetables into a pint jar.

In a small saucepan over medium heat, combine **½ cup [120 ml] of unseasoned rice vinegar** and **6 tablespoons [90 g] of sugar**. Stir until the sugar dissolves, about 1 to 2 minutes.

Pour the brine over the vegetables and cover the jar with a tight lid.

Let the pickle sit on the countertop for at least 1 hour before eating it. This pickle can be refrigerated for up to 1 month.

PICKLE FACT

The Christmas Pickle. Don't pretend you've never heard of it. The tradition of hiding a pickle (or in modern times, a pickle ornament) in the Christmas tree has been amusing holiday enthusiasts and piquant picklers for centuries. Here's how it works: A small gherkin is hung and hidden amid the green twigs of the decorated pine. Sharp-eyed family members compete to be the first to spot it. In return, they get good luck for the year—and/or in some families, they're the first to open their gifts. This little ritual is often credited to the Germans, but it's more likely to have stemmed from German immigrants in the midwestern United States.

Thai Cucumber Quickle

Quick + Pickle = Quickle! If you are pickle curious and you have only a single toe to dip in the food preservation arts, let this simple recipe be the one to make you pucker. Quickles take only minutes to throw together, and they are ready to eat in about an hour. Voila! You've found it! The shortest path to pickles.

Cut **1 hothouse or English cucumber** (seeds removed) and **1 small red onion** into thin slices. In a medium bowl, combine the cucumber and onion with **2 teaspoons of sugar**, **2 teaspoons of kosher salt**, and **½ cup [120 ml] of distilled white vinegar**. Toss and let stand for 1 hour.

You can eat your quickles immediately or store them in the refrigerator, where they'll keep for about 1 week.

Coconut Cilantro Chutney

Lines can get blurry between a pickle, a condiment, and a chutney. While pickles tend to be made with preservation and longevity in mind, chutneys can be made for long-term storage or fresh use. This is a fresh chutney, but it's so delicious that it warranted its place in this book. It's meaty and rich from the coconut, and it has a lot of flavors in a small bite thanks to the lemon, fresh herbs, and chiles. If you don't have a high tolerance for spicy food, feel free to swap out the serrano chile with a jalapeño or omit it altogether. This is great next to any kind of seafood and rice.

cont'd.

In a food processor, finely mince **1⅓ cups [125 g] of unsweetened flaked coconut**, **1 small serrano chile** (stem removed), **¼ cup [5 g] of packed fresh mint**, **¼ cup [5 g] of packed fresh cilantro**, **2 tablespoons of fresh lemon juice**, and **¾ teaspoon of kosher salt** for about 3 minutes, scraping down the sides as needed. Add up to ½ cup [120 ml] of water, a little at a time, until the consistency is cohesive and spoonable.

Meanwhile, in a small skillet over medium heat, warm **2 tablespoons of canola or grapeseed oil**. Add **1 tablespoon of cumin seeds** and toast them until the seeds become light brown and fragrant, about 2 to 3 minutes. Add the seeds and every bit of the oil to the food processor. Give it a whirl on high, scraping down the sides as needed, to mix everything thoroughly.

Serve the chutney immediately. Leftovers can be refrigerated but must be eaten within a few days.

PICKLE FACT

Salt is imperative to pickles. It adds flavor, helps protect from spoilage, and pulls moisture out of the vegetable. Pickling salt does not contain anti-caking ingredients, which can turn pickling liquid cloudy, or additives like iodine, which can make pickles dark. In addition, pickling salt has fine granules that make it easy to dissolve in a brine. That said, you don't *have* to use pickling salt. Diamond Crystal kosher salt or sea salt can also be used, but they aren't interchangeable.

Scorched Red Peppers and Celery

Yes, celery. It's so, so good for pickling because of its crunch and its natural saltiness. And it's time that this second-class vegetable got its moment centerplate. People often complain about the texture of celery, but if you peel it like a carrot and remove those tough strings, everyone changes their tune. And do you know what balances out celery perfectly? Sweet red peppers made even sweeter because you've caramelized them. Try these two together. They will be the stars of your next meal.

cont'd.

Use a vegetable peeler to peel **1 pound [455 g] of celery**, then slice the celery at an angle, ¾ inches thick. Transfer to a medium bowl.

Heat **1 tablespoon of olive oil** in a skillet over medium-high heat. Add **2 medium red bell peppers**, cut into long strips, and **2 teaspoons of kosher salt**. Sauté until the pepper softens and blackens in spots, 7 to 8 minutes.

Add the bell pepper to the celery, along with **3 teaspoons of sugar**, **⅓ cup [80 ml] of extra virgin olive oil**, **½ cup [120 ml] of distilled white vinegar**, ⅓ cup [80 ml] of water, **8 sprigs of fresh oregano**, and **1 minced garlic clove**. Toss to combine.

Pack the pickle into jars or a container with a tight-fitting lid and refrigerate. Don't worry if it looks like there's not enough brine; liquid will pull from the vegetables as they sit. Wait 1 day before eating. Kept cold, this pickle will last at least 1 month.

PICKLE FACT

Some delicious and slightly unusual pickled things to try include fried pickles dipped in aioli, guacamole studded with chopped pickles, Polish pickle soup, a pickleback chaser after a shot of mezcal or whiskey, and a pickle and peanut butter sandwich. I cannot eat a hamburger or tuna salad without pickles, and neither should you.

British Pub Pickle

A ploughman's lunch is a bowl or jar of this pickle served with crusty bread, sharp cheddar cheese, spicy cured sausage, hard-boiled eggs, pickled onions, and a cold beer. Or some combination thereof. The pickle is the high point of the meal, though—sweet, tangy, and full of vegetables and fruit.

One note on the tamarind paste: if you can find it, buy the stuff in a jar that's ready to use—much less mess. If you can't find it, buy a block of tamarind, soak a big square of it in warm water, remove the skins and pods, and then squish it to make a paste.

Peel, prep, and finely dice **1 to 2 carrots** (about 1½ cups [300 g]), **¼ of a head of cauliflower** (about 1 cup [340 g]), **1 to 2 zucchini** (about 1 cup [340 g]), and **1 medium red onion** (about 1 cup [140 g]). Set aside.

cont'd.

Make the brine. In a large, heavy-bottomed saucepan or Dutch oven, boil **16 finely chopped Medjool dates** (pits removed), **2 medium sweet apples** (peeled, cored, and finely diced), **4 thinly sliced garlic cloves**, **3½ cups [840 ml] of apple cider vinegar**, **2 cups [400 g] of sugar**, **½ cup [120 g] of tamarind paste**, and **1 tablespoon of kosher salt**. Note that the volume of the liquid will increase when it boils.

Reduce the heat and simmer, uncovered, for about 30 minutes, mashing the fruit with a wooden spoon or potato masher as it softens. Scrape the bottom and sides of the saucepan to keep it from sticking. Once the volume of the liquid has reduced by half and the mixture has become somewhat thick and syrupy, turn off the heat.

Add the vegetables to the pot and stir to combine. Let the pickle cool at room temperature for about 1 hour.

Pack the pickle into glass jars or a container with a tight-fitting lid. Refrigerated, this will keep for at least 2 months.

PICKLE FACT

While pickles are most commonly enjoyed straight from jar to mouth, cooking with pickles is a joy. Sure, you can toss them cold into a green salad, egg salad, potato salad, and the like—and you absolutely will not be disappointed. But melted into a grilled cheese or on top of pizza? Heaven. The brine frozen into a popsicle, with or without diced fresh fruit? That's pure cool on a hot day. And if you just can't get enough brine, ladle up a bowl of Polish pickle soup—a creamy potato soup enhanced with bright dill and the acidic bite of dill pickles.

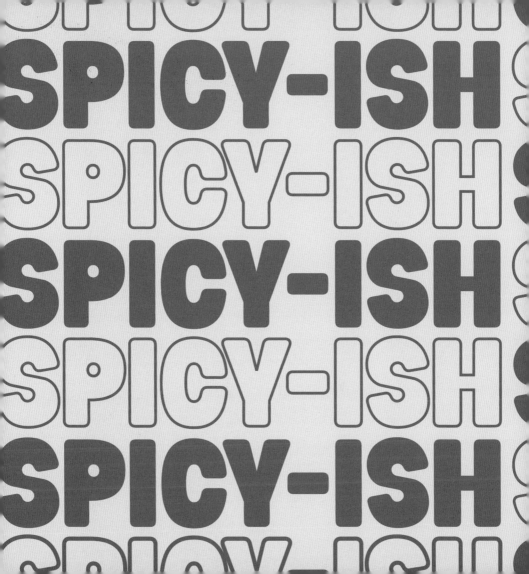

Everyday Fire Sauce

Some meals just aren't complete without hot sauce. If you put fried rice, tacos, or red beans and rice in front of me and there's no hot sauce in the house, I'm going out for pizza (which I don't usually put hot sauce on, but I'm not opposed to it). Without exaggeration, as I write this, there are no fewer than a dozen fiery bottles and jars in my refrigerator door. And with this recipe, there will be thirteen. Please take caution when handling these (or any) hot peppers. Gloves and goggles are a good idea. The oils from the peppers can travel from your hands to anything else you touch.

cont'd.

Working in two batches, blend **2 pounds [910 g] of Fresno peppers** (for red sauce) or jalapeños (for green sauce), **6 garlic cloves**, and **2 teaspoons of fine-grain sea salt** in a food processor until it has the consistency of a smoothie—about 2 minutes. Some foam may appear on top.

Scrape the sauce into a very clean 1 quart [945 ml] or larger glass jar or transparent container. You don't want plastic, as it will retain the strong odors. Cover the top of the jar loosely with a small square of clean cloth or a piece of paper towel and secure it in place with a rubber band. You want the sauce to have access to the air but keep out insects and debris.

Keep the jar in a cool spot away from direct sunlight to ferment for 4 to 7 days. The sauce will separate, and the thick part will bubble when it ferments. Taste it. If you'd like to develop the fermented flavor, let it sit for another week or so.

Strain the fermented sauce through a fine-mesh sieve and discard the solids (or use them to flavor a stir-fry or marinade). Add **3 tablespoons of distilled white vinegar** and stir to combine.

If you have a shaker-top jar, it's a great fit for your hot sauce. Kept covered and refrigerated, this sauce will keep for at least 2 months.

Spicy Escabeche

This is the mandatory spicy accompaniment to all future tacos. While excellent with the traditional green jalapeño, feel free to take advantage of other hot peppers, such as bright red Fresnos, mild pasillas, or fiery habañeros.

Cut **7 medium carrots** into ½ inch [13 mm] rounds. Cut **7 large jalapeño peppers** into ¼ inch [6 mm] rounds. Slice **1 medium white onion** into ¼ inch [6 mm] strips.

In a medium saucepan over high heat, bring **1½ cups [360 ml] of distilled white vinegar**, 2 cups [480 ml] of water, **2 tablespoons of kosher salt**, ¼ cup [40 g] of sugar, and **1 tablespoon of dried oregano** to a boil. Stir to dissolve the sugar and mix the spices.

Add the carrots, peppers, and onion to the boiling brine. Stir to coat the vegetables and gently press them down into the brine to cover them completely.

cont'd.

Reduce the heat to medium, cover, and simmer the vegetables for 12 to 15 minutes, stirring occasionally, until the carrots are just tender. Don't overcook this; no one likes a mushy pickle.

If you have three 1 pint [475 ml] canning jars, divide **6 lightly crushed garlic cloves**, **3 bay leaves**, and **1 tablespoon of black peppercorns** into the bottom of each jar. (If you don't have canning jars, put the garlic, bay leaves, and peppercorns into a large container with a tight-fitting lid.)

Divide the carrots, peppers, and onions evenly between each jar and then cover with brine completely.

Marinate the pickles for at least 12 hours before eating them. This pickle will keep for at least 4 months in the refrigerator.

Spicy Blackened Szechuan Pickled Peppers

These puckery peppers pack heat, tang, and pungency. Some of the flavors here are truly unique, including the unexpected herbaceous, floral kick of Szechuan peppercorns—they taste like nothing else. And a bit of liquor in the brine really gives these pickles an edge. Note that in a Chinese grocery story you will find both Shaoxing wine and Shaoxing cooking wine. Be sure to use the former as it's of higher quality and has a much cleaner flavor.

cont'd.

Wash **16 whole**, **fresh Fresno chiles** and trim off the stems. Use a toothpick to stab six holes around the stem end of the fruit.

In a medium Dutch oven (or any heavy-bottomed pot large enough to hold all the peppers in a single layer) heat **1 teaspoon of peanut oil** over high heat. Add the peppers in a single layer and sear them for about 7 to 8 minutes, rolling them around until they blacken in spots.

Reduce the heat to medium and add **½ teaspoon of Szechuan peppercorns** to the pot. Stir them in with the peppers for another 3 minutes until fragrant.

Add **1 cup [240 ml] of distilled white vinegar**, 1 cup [240 ml] of water, **3 thin slices of fresh ginger**, **2 smashed garlic cloves**, **5 teaspoons of sugar**, and **1½ teaspoons of kosher salt**. Stir to combine and gently simmer, uncovered, for 5 minutes to let the peppers soften.

Turn off the heat. When the bubbling subsides, add **⅓ cup [80 ml] of Shaoxing wine or gin** and stir.

Transfer the peppers and their brine to a clean jar (or another container) with a tight lid. Let it sit on the countertop for 24 hours before refrigerating. Eat after 3 days. Kept cold, this pickle will last about 1 month.

PICKLE FACT

Cultures all the world over make pickles—and for good reason. It's a way to preserve food during times of agricultural surplus and save it for later. In the winter months when fresh vegetables are nonexistent, pickled vegetables are an important source of vitamins and fiber. They add crunch and acidity to a meal, making them a great food to help with both digestion and to stimulate the appetite. Historically, pickles also helped disguise less palatable flavors such as less-than-fresh meat. Not to mention, pickles are the original fast food! They're a perfect snack for eating on the go.

Spicy Pickled Pineapple Salsa

Pickling fruit is a wild act in a world of vegetable dominance. And pineapple is one of the best built for brine. It's firm, naturally acidic, and sweet, so it holds its own in a vinegar or fermented bath. In this pickle, the heat from the sriracha balances out that tropical sweetness, and its red flecks pop against the sunny yellow fruit. This pickle is a lifesaver if fresh pineapples are out of season.

If you're buying fish sauce for the first time, my favorite brand is Red Boat. If you can't find that, look for a product with simple, non-chemical ingredients—it should contain only fish and salt. To keep this vegan, swap it out with Bragg Liquid Aminos.

cont'd.

In a food processor, pulse **1 garlic clove** until it is finely minced. Add **½ of a fresh small pineapple** (skinned and core removed) and pulse until the fruit is in pea-size chunks. Note that if you don't have a food processor, you can do the knife work to finely mince the garlic and the fruit.

Transfer the pineapple and garlic to a medium mixing bowl. Stir in **1½ teaspoons of kosher salt**, **2 tablespoons of sriracha**, **2 tablespoons of fish sauce**, and **½ cup [120 ml] of distilled white vinegar**.

Spoon the salsa into a jar or any container with a tight-fitting lid. Cover with a lid and let it sit at least 1 hour before eating. Stored in the refrigerator, this salsa will continue to be delicious for at least 2 weeks.

Javanese Acar Timun

A version of this simple Javanese carrot and cucumber pickle is also eaten in Malaysia and Singapore—and its wide appeal is easy to understand. It's crunchy and pretty, and has a nice bite from shallots, a sweet edge from sugar, a light hand of vinegar, and a mild jab of chiles. It's a must-eat with chicken satay or fried food of any kind, and it's the quintessential pickle of Indonesian national dishes nasi goreng (fried rice) and mie goreng (fried noodles). Eat this as is or top it with ground macadamia nuts before serving.

cont'd.

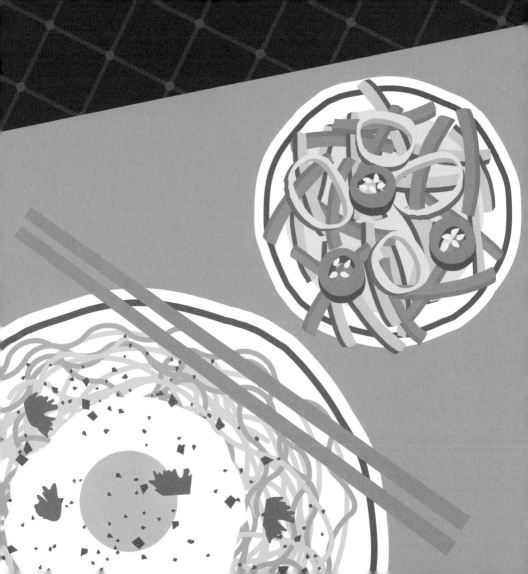

Julienne **5 medium carrots** and **3 small Persian cucumbers**. In a medium mixing bowl, toss the vegetables with **1½ teaspoons of kosher salt**. Let them sit for 10 minutes, tossing occasionally.

In the meantime, slice **2 large shallots** and **1 large jalapeño** into thin rings. Set aside.

After the carrots and cucumbers have sweated out some moisture, drain and squeeze them very firmly until no further liquid rains out. Put them back in the bowl and add the shallots and jalapeño. Toss to combine.

Pack the vegetables into canning jars or any container with a tight-fitting lid.

Make the brine. In a small saucepan, combine **¾ cup [180 ml] of distilled white vinegar**, 1½ cups [360 ml] of water, and **¼ cup [40 g] of sugar**. Bring to a boil, stirring to dissolve the sugar.

Pour the boiling brine over the vegetables to cover, pressing down on the vegetables as needed to help them submerge. Cover the jar with the lid and let it sit on the countertop for 24 hours before eating this pickle. Covered and refrigerated, the acar timun will last at least 3 weeks.

Kimchi

This is the de facto national pickle—and national pride—of Korea. This recipe makes a good-size batch, and I encourage you to taste it fresh, and then keep tasting it often to notice how its flavors and textures change and develop. When you're ready to eat it, note that kitchen shears, and not a knife and cutting board, are the best way to cut your cabbage down to size without letting that delicious liquid escape. If you don't live near a Korean grocery store, you can order gochu-jang (Korean chili paste) and gochugaru (Korean chili flakes) online.

Start with **5 pounds [2.3 kg] of napa cabbage**, usually 1 or 2 heads. Discard the tough outer leaves. Cut the cabbage in half lengthwise just through the base (leaving the root intact). Then, with your hands, pull up from the base to tear the upper leaves into two halves. Lay the flat side

cont'd.

down, cut the cabbage in half again at the base, then pull the quarters apart with your hands. You should have 4 to 8 long quarters of cabbage, depending on how many heads you started with.

Measure **½ cup [150 g] of Maldon sea salt** into a small dish. (For this recipe, it's important to use Maldon if possible. It has a very big flake, so the measurements will be off if you use standard sea salt.) Working with one cabbage quarter at a time, lightly sprinkle salt between the leaves, concentrating on the bottom leaves closest to the root. As you finish salting the cabbage, line the quarters up "head to toe," cut-side up, in a 9 by 13 [23 by 33 cm] baking dish. Pack them snugly; if they don't all fit, you can let a couple of the quarters rest on top of the others.

Place something flat, such as a cutting board, a serving plate, or a smaller baking dish, on top of the cabbage. Add 5 pounds [2.3 kg] of weight on top of that object to further press down the cabbage. If you don't have a small hand weight, you can use heavy cans or jars full of liquid.

After 30 minutes, flip the pieces over so they're cut-side down, replace the board and the weight, and let the cabbage sit for another 30 minutes.

While the cabbage is being pressed, make the sauce. In a small saucepan over high heat, boil 1½ cups [360 ml] of water.

Whisk in **3 tablespoons of sweet rice flour** or all-purpose flour and lower the heat to a simmer, whisking constantly for 1 to 2 minutes until it's smooth and thick.

Turn off the heat. Add **¼ cup [60 ml] of Korean chili paste** (gochujang), **2 tablespoons of sugar**, and **¾ cup [50 g] of Korean chili flakes** (gochugaru). Whisk to combine.

In the work bowl of a food processor fitted with a metal blade, pulse **10 large garlic cloves** and a **2 inch [5 cm] knob of ginger** until finely minced. Add the cooked flour slurry, along with **2 tablespoons of fish sauce**, and process on high until fully smooth, about 1 minute.

Uncover the salted cabbage and hold each quarter up by its root end over the dish. Squeeze the excess moisture from the cabbage with your hands and lay the drained cabbage quarters onto a plate. Discard whatever liquid has puddled in the bottom of the dish.

Working with one cabbage quarter at a time, spoon about 1 to 1½ teaspoons of the sauce between each leaf, starting at the root end and working your way up. Don't worry if the sauce does not fully coat the leafy tops. Return the cabbage to the baking dish, pack the quarters in "head to toe" once again, this time stuffing all the cabbage (now much more flexible) into a single layer.

cont'd.

If there's any remaining sauce, spoon it on top of the cabbage. Use your hands to work the sauce into the top of the leaves, and roll the cabbage around to fully coat it on all sides.

Now pack the kimchi to let it ferment. Place a layer of plastic wrap directly, but loosely, on top of the kimchi, leaving room for contact with the air along the sides. Replace the board and the 5 pound [2.3 kg] weight.

Cover the weighted kimchi loosely with a clean kitchen towel to keep out insects and debris but let air flow in. Let the cabbage rest in a cool, dark place for 4 to 6 days, until it takes on a pleasantly fermented odor. Don't worry if you see liquid pooling in the bottom of the baking dish; this is part of the process.

Once it has fermented to your liking, your kimchi is ready to eat. To serve, you can cut up one cabbage quarter at a time to serve it in smaller pieces, or simply trim off and discard the root ends for longer pieces.

For storage, pack the kimchi tightly into pickling jars or an airtight container (glass or ceramic is best) with a tight-fitting lid and refrigerate. Your kimchi will last at least 6 weeks, but it will soften over time. After that, if the texture is too soft, you can use it for cooking (in soup, fried rice, scrambled eggs, or Korean pancakes) for at least another 6 weeks.

PICKLE
FACT

November 22 is Kimchi Day in
Korea. Traditionally, families
come together to batch their
kimchi supply for the year—
which is a lot of kimchi! Not
only does kimchi taste great,
but it's built to last. Spicy
chiles, ginger, garlic, and
salt are all naturally anti-
microbial, meaning they help
prevent food from spoiling.

Green Mango Pickle

Unripe mango, like unripe papaya, makes fine, firm, puckery pickles. The texture of the mango is yielding and squash-like. Leaving the skin intact helps give this a nice bite, and the warm Indian spices really make the bright flavors sing. Dollop it by the spoonful next to your curry and rice. Or stir it into plain yogurt. It's refreshing and heavily spiced enough to wake up your mouth between bites of anything rich and fatty.

Chop **1 large unripe mango** into ½ inch [13 mm] cubes. You should have about 2½ cups [350 g] of cut fruit.

cont'd.

In a medium skillet over medium heat, warm **¼ cup [60 ml] of grapeseed oil** (or any neutral oil) and stir in **1 tablespoon of cumin seed**, **1 tablespoon of chili powder**, **2 teaspoons of fenugreek seed**, and **3 thinly sliced garlic cloves**. Cook for about 4 minutes, stirring frequently, until the spices become fragrant and the garlic browns.

Add the mango to the skillet, stir to combine, and cook for an additional 3 minutes until the fruit becomes slightly soft.

Turn off the heat. Add **2 teaspoons of kosher salt**, **2 teaspoons of asafetida**, **1 teaspoon of ground turmeric**, **2 tablespoons of light brown sugar**, and **¼ cup [60 ml] of distilled white vinegar** to the skillet. Mix thoroughly.

Pack the pickle into jars or any container with a tight-fitting lid (avoid plastic, as it will retain this pickle's color and strong perfume). This pickle can be eaten immediately, but it is better if you allow it to sit at room temperature for 24 hours.

Refrigerated, this pickle will last for at least 4 months.

Harissa Mixed Pickle

Harissa is a spicy chili paste common in North African and Middle Eastern cooking. You can make your own, but it's also easy to buy a good-quality harissa; just look for simple ingredients, such as various types of chiles, garlic, olive oil, vinegar, and warm spices like cumin, coriander, and caraway. Harissa can range in flavor and heat level, so taste it before you use it.

Cut **½ of a head of cauliflower** into 1 inch pieces. Cut **1 to 2 carrots** into 1 inch rounds. Cut **2 to 3 celery stalks** into 1 inch pieces. You should end up with about 1 cup [120 g] of each vegetable.

cont'd.

In a large mixing bowl, combine the vegetables. Then pack them into a jar or another container with a tight-fitting lid and add **1 crushed garlic clove**.

In a medium saucepan, boil **1¼ cup [300 ml] of distilled white vinegar**, ¾ cup [180 ml] of water, **2 tablespoons of kosher salt**, **2 tablespoons of sugar**, **2 teaspoons of ground turmeric**, and **2 tablespoons of harissa paste**. Stir to dissolve the ingredients.

Pour the hot brine over the vegetables and cover the jar with its lid.

Let the pickle sit at room temperature for 24 hours, then move the jar to the refrigerator. Let it sit at least 2 days before eating. Refrigerated, this pickle will keep for at least 3 weeks.

Acknowledgments

Thank you so much to every farmworker who has put in the long hours and backbreaking work to grow the fruits and vegetables that I buy every week at the San Francisco Bay Area's many farmers' markets. Or, for that matter, anyone who grows healthy food or contributes to our underappreciated healthy food systems. Thank you. I mean it. Just buying from you is not enough. You stand atop the podium of good people.

Thank you also to the people who made this book possible. Alex Galou at Chronicle Books has been the driving force behind the project, unfathomably patient, and entirely too kind and receptive. You're a pleasure to work with, and I would jump at the chance to do it again.

Thanks also to my agent, Danielle Svetcov. You've been there from the very, very beginning, and I am always delighted to work with you, to have you tell me how it is, and for a brief moment long ago, it was a pleasure to be your neighbor. Thank you for all that you've done for me these past fifteen years. I am always delighted for your continued success.

I thank my nesting partners and main squeeze pickle-tasters Matthew, Emmett, Desmond, Doug Rambo, and Ginger. You make life more fun and more delicious. I love you all.

And last but not least, I'd like to thank everyone who has been in touch about my books and events. Please keep your comments and kitchen trials and tribulations coming to me at ksolomon.com.